YOUR KNOWLEDGE HAS VALUE

- We will publish your bachelor's and master's thesis, essays and papers

- Your own eBook and book - sold worldwide in all relevant shops

- Earn money with each sale

Upload your text at www.GRIN.com and publish for free

Marcio Hemerique Pereira

Natural Beauty and Art Beauty: Kant, Hegel and Adorno revisited

GRIN Verlag

Bibliografische Information der Deutschen Nationalbibliothek:

Die Deutsche Bibliothek verzeichnet diese Publikation in der Deutschen National-
bibliografie; detaillierte bibliografische Daten sind im Internet über http://dnb.d-
nb.de/ abrufbar.

Imprint:

Copyright © 2011 GRIN Verlag GmbH
Druck und Bindung: Books on Demand GmbH, Norderstedt Germany
ISBN: 978-3-656-34899-3

GRIN - Your knowledge has value

Der GRIN Verlag publiziert seit 1998 wissenschaftliche Arbeiten von Studenten, Hochschullehrern und anderen Akademikern als eBook und gedrucktes Buch. Die Verlagswebsite www.grin.com ist die ideale Plattform zur Veröffentlichung von Hausarbeiten, Abschlussarbeiten, wissenschaftlichen Aufsätzen, Dissertationen und Fachbüchern.

Visit us on the internet:

http://www.grin.com/

http://www.facebook.com/grincom

http://www.twitter.com/grin_com

NATURAL BEAUTY AND ART BEAUTY:

KANT, HEGEL AND ADORNO REVISITED

Marcio Hemerique Pereira

Birkbeck College

University of London

[...] The true purpose of painting is to represent objects as they really are; that is to say, differently from the way we see them. It tends always to give us their sensible essence, their presence, this is why the image it forms does not resemble their appearance [...][1]

The present essay proposes to compare and contrast the relationship between natural beauty and art beauty as it is conceived by Kant, Hegel and Adorno.[2] Exploring these forms intrinsically attached to public and private concerns of the Aesthetics Theory, I will try to go beyond the author's texts and understand, if not explore, what they intended to say to the society and the implications it had in our society after that. Equally important, relate their works in Aesthetics and inside-out world. Finally, the essay tangles the different efforts of the writers when using representative forms of speech and what considers being a more viable and broader definition of that Aesthetics.

---

[1] Jacques Rivière (1886-1924) *'Present Tendencies in Painting'* p. 190. In *Art in Theory* (1900-2000). *An Anthology of Changing Ideas.* Ed. by Charles Harrison & Paul Wood. Blackwell Publishing, 2002.

[2] Hegel considered that the artistic beauty as the defining characteristic of works of art while Adorno considered it as the moment that turns an artefact into art and determines its greatness. Kant on the other hand considered that some beauty does not express a function at all, but it depends entirely on how the thing is considered in itself. These considerations are referred to in: Kant, *Critique Judgment*, transl. Meredith (Oxford: Oxford University Press), section 16. Theodor Adorno, *Aesthetic Theory*, trans. C. Lenhardt (New York: Routledge & Kegan Paul, 1984), p.16. Georg Wilhelm Friedrich Hegel, "*The Philosophy of Fine Arts*," in *Philosophies of Art and Beauty*, ed. Albert Hofstadter and Richard Kughns (New York: The Modern Library, 1964), p.30.

Natural Beauty and Art Beauty

Beauty is an element which gives pleasure to the human beings. The concept of beauty is found in different cultures with a lot of features.[3] Hegel, Adorno and Kant were great modern philosophers with their concepts on Beauty of Art and Beauty of Nature. Hegelian philosophy declares that true beautiful is divine creature in material shape that finds out beauty in fine art and he keeps out the beauty of nature. Aftermath of Kant, the concept of natural beautiful is turned down mainly because of the arguments of Hegel for the beauty of art. He affirms that a simple art work pass through individuals mind is superior to any creation of nature. Adorno considers realistic beauty happens through the ability of a person to access the object in its distinctiveness. He was inspired by Kant so one can see this influence in his notion. Adorno acquired some support from Kant for his idea of beauty.

However Adorno, says that there is an evil star hangs over the concept of natural beauty. Kant claims that the beautiful should recognize with purposive, but not any specific purpose. But art works have definite purposes given by the artists while their production, that is, beauty is the spirit forms through the judgment of mind.[4]

The discussion on the relation between artistic beauty and natural beauty started from the time of the 'Critique of Judgment' introduced by Immanuel Kant. Nature plays an imperative role in his explanation of beauty. Philosophical suggestions on the art and nature were shifted in the direction of a philosophy of fine art mainly by the arguments put forwarded by the German philosopher Hegel. Kant claimed that the superior structure of beauty is free and self-regulating[5] but Hegel

---

[3] Jacob (quoted by Matineau) says, "The beautiful has this feature, in common with all that is original, that there is no mark by which we know it. It exists and is self-manifest; you show it but not prove it – *es kan gewiesen, aber nicht bewiesen weiden*."

[4] Immanuel Kant, *Critique of Judgment*, Translated by Werner S. Pluhar, Hackett Publishing Co., 1987

[5] Kant recognizes, and gives special treatment to, four classes of beautiful objects: free beauty, dependent beauty, beauty in art, beauty in nature. Kant also recognizes two kinds of judgments of taste: pure judgments of taste (the object of which is always free beauty) and impure judgments of taste (the objects of which is always dependent beauty). This point can easily accessed in Eva Schaper in "*Free and Dependent Beauty*," which is chapter 3 of *Studies in Kant's Aesthetics* (Edinburgh: Edinburgh University Press, 1979).

persisted that, to obvious beauty of art is superior to all that is exterior. He used the possibilities of spiritual elements with his scientific view point to define beauty. By a reasonable scientific treatment, his spiritualization of content keeps out the natural beauty. One can see same attitude in the writings of Kant and Hegel but it only in their hierarchical arrangement that consider the relation connecting natural beauty and artistic beauty. Kant considered natural beauty as greater than artificial beauty but according to Hegel the beauty of art is better than the beauty of nature. At the same time 20th century philosopher Theodor W. Adorno, changed their hierarchies related with the idea of beauty. Ástráður Eysteinsson and Vivian Liska, for instance, pointed out that, "Adorno occupies a modernist position in the area of aesthetics because he breaks Hegel's ideals of artistic harmony" (Eysteinsson, 2004, p.144). In his 'Aesthetic Theory,' Adorno explains that natural beauty is not a superior one over artistic beauty. He argues that natural beauty is a prerequisite for the positive treatment of artistic beauty. Adorno recognizes the aesthetic skill of nature and also positively consider aesthetic experience of art works. Thus he made a synthesis between Kant and Hegel to clearly define the concept of beauty. In short Adorno's attempt was to avoid the bias of Kant and Hegel towards the realization of beauty.

*

Aesthetics concept of Hegel is regarded as one of the greatest theories made after Aristotle. Like other many German philosophers Hegel was also a child of neoclassical approach and looked back to the ancient classical age of Europe. Hegel was understood about the setback which continued his own period also.[6] Consequently, he supported that the artist should take theme from the ancient time. His philosophy related with beauty is influenced several thinkers and he was very exact regarding the type of art to find out beauty. His principles on aesthetics are comprehensive notions of beauty and ideal. Beauty in art is the production of the spirit or truth through an object and it can identify only by a deep form called the 'ideal' that transcends it to a special form. Beardsley states that, "The artistically embodied idea, Hegel calls 'Ideal" (Beardsley, 1975, p. 237). On the opposite, spirit is only the true, realizing everything in itself, and then one can say that all are truly

---

[6] William Desmond, Art and the Absolute: A Study of Hegel's Aesthetics. (Albany: State University of New York Press, 1986).

3

beautiful only as distribution in this superior sphere and made by it. Hegel puts forward his argument about beauty. He exclusively finds out beauty in fine art and he totally keeps out the beauty of nature. According to Hegel, the idea is constantly opposite to Nature and the mind generates art, which provides idea to nature. Moreover, he considers beauty in nature is too formless and there are no criteria to analyze it. In addition he argues that a silly fancy pass through a person's mind is superior to any creation of nature. This constant difference between beauty of art and beauty of nature is a vital point.[7] Thus, Hegel inserts into the history of aesthetics against the concept of Kant which is more recognized beauty of nature.

Carritt writes that, "Hegel refuses to consider nature as strictly beautiful, and defines aesthetic as the philosophy of fine art" (Carritt, 1962, p. 102). Hegel is profoundly making a scientific and an objective study of beauty and in the second chapter of 'Lecture on Aesthetics'. He observes that recent concepts of beauty pointed a dichotomy between the representation of beauty and content. This dichotomy involves that a basic element of the beautiful.

**

Hegel considered art as a creation of individuals' freedom; it places in opposition to the nature. In Hegel's opinion art must be a free creation, that should show freedom above the concept of beauty and truth that is the property of an artist's free mind. He explains that nature becomes beautiful only through the art work of man. So he argues that beauty is the result of human freedom and it is distinctive from the beauty of nature. In Hegel's opinion Painting is the most appropriate expression of the mind, spirit and personality of the artist. Painting is an imaginative manifestation, rather than reality or substance and here the mental process of an artist is the determining factor, it is purposive with all significance. However Hegel could not consider a sculpture that was permitted to surpass nature into idealism. Sculpture was, regardless of its attempt more bound to the "real." Hegel's philosophy related with beauty becomes distinctive because of his concentration on the content of fine art. He makes a clear distinction between beauty of art and beauty of nature.

---

[7] G. W. F. Hegel, *Aesthetics: Lectures on Fine Art*. Chapters on 'Natural beauty' and 'Art Beauty' in part I [In volume 1 of the Knox translation]. Full reference is given in the end of this essay.

4

He used a particular term aesthetic to identify his interest in the philosophy of fine art. Sukla stated that, "Mind and artistic beauty stands higher than natural beauty but this distinction is simply relative" (Sukla, 2003, p. 51). His content in fine art is called by him as the 'Idea' and it is considered as truth. He describes that the supreme or universal spirit acquires knowledge to there. Thus Hegelian philosophy tells that the true beautiful is divine creature in material shape through the artist and the content of this world is the beautiful. The Ideal in Hegel's opinion cannot inevitably be understood however he recognizes an art work as more beautiful and more profound is content; its inner truth. The beauty reveals the function of art and it is the truth. Hegel recognizes that art can help or instruct mankind that art is an end in itself as result it is not a way something additional. Thus concept of art for art's sake was a reasonably new one introduced by Hegel and widely accepts it. But Kant's writings on aesthetics often try to connect beauty with ethics.

Adorno emphasizes that beauty is taken into the custody in the "unconscious consciousness, in the middle of the effort itself. He considers true beauty happens when there acquires the ability of a person to access the object with its distinctiveness. Angus Nicholls and Martin Liebscher remark that, "He realizes that without this moment of unconscious nearness the investment in aesthetic beauty, which is based on its offering a sense of otherwise inaccessible, meaning, is inexplicable" (Nicholls and Liebscher, 2010, p. 83). In this sense one can consider him as a supporter of Kantian ideology. But Adorno is a negative Kantian because he emphasizes the way of concepts set against a person from the world. This way is different from Kant's approach that permits a person to capture it. This transcendence of the theoretical is an open response in opposition to Kantian artistic idea. It is a true that Adorno has inspired by Kant so it is hard to keep away from his notion. In effect Adorno obtained some encouragement from Kant for his idea of beauty. At the same time it is a significant feature of Kantian beauty that it is not directed by a particular concept, it accepts involvement of the application of ideals to the sensory manifold. Natural beauty according to Adorno, was passed over in agreement of art beauty. As the suitable subject matter of aesthetics freedom and ascendancy of the balanced subject were designated in art, not nature. Nicholsen says that, "Natural beauty seems to stand apart from the subjective perceiver and to be independent from it" (Nicholsen, 1999, p. 159). This was devastating because the notion of the topic as free and consistent. It became a vital aspect of the period of thinking, identity and consequently the regular purpose of Adorno's analysis.

On the name of false dichotomy between art and natural beauty, Adorno criticizes Hegel. According to him Hegel saw art beauty as superior to natural beauty and as less theoretically interfere than art beauty. But Adorno identifies that in both cases individuals experience is totally mediate by individuals concepts. Thus Adorno argues that Hegel chalks up as the insufficiency of natural beauty. The feature of escaping from unchanging concept is however the material of beauty itself. With regard to art beauty and natural beauty Adorno does not seek to carry out any sort of shrinking. It not says that there is no sense in which natural beauty and art beauty are separate; certainly, there are many different ways. In general, spirit plays a prominent role in describing ascetic beauty. Adorno points out it as the moment that turns an artifact into art and deciding its importance. But Hegel considered spirit as the determining feature of works of art that provides beauty to it. According to Adorno spirit is too significant factor in the creation of natural beauty. At the same time, Hegel argues spirit is not associated with nature. The disregard of natural beauty follows from the following pattern, for the work of art, being a product of the human spirit, always goes further than any product of nature:

> "In virtue of emotion and insight in the atmosphere of which landscape is portrayed by the art of painting, this creation of human spirit assumes the higher rank than the purely natural landscape. Everything which partakes of spirit is better than anything, begotten of mere nature. [...] no purely natural existence is able, as art is, to represent divine ideals [...] and to endow with permanence [...]"[8]

Adorno says that, "Art is not infiltrated by spirit; rather spirit, follows art works where they want to go, setting free their immanent language" (Adorno, 1997, p. 92).

***

---

[8] Georg Wilhelm Friedrich Hegel, "*The philosophy of Fine Arts*." Op. cit. p. 300.

Immanuel Kant is one of the most prominent philosophers of the Enlightenment period. He is an ideal for everyone as the realm of philosophy first time and in all related disciplines.[9] His brilliance and experience are associated closely in the notion of beauty. Later, his concepts are followed and criticized by several thinkers like Hegel and Adorno. In 1764, he published his '*Observations on the Feeling of the Beautiful and the Sublime*' and in 1790, published his important Critique, '*The Critique of the Power of Judgment.*' His aesthetics concepts offer new approaching for old problems regarding to define beauty. It describes feeling, experience, pleasure, subjectivity, aesthetic ideas, and beauty of nature in opposition to beauty of art. Through the question 'how are judgments about beauty possible', Kant begins to examine the knowledge of beauty with his new concepts about beauty of nature. Stephen Davies, Kathleen Marie Higgins and Robert Hopkins write that, "Kant has some sharp reasons for setting them aside in judgments of pure beauty" (Davies, *et al*, 2009, p. 51). His first focal point is on judgments regarding beauty in nature, as when we identify a bird, an animal or a sunset 'beautiful'. Kant needs to make clear the fundamental features of judgments related with how does a person has effect beauty as a mental work. Aesthetic judgments according to Kant's analysis are extraordinary even than normal reflective judgments. His judgments have several peculiar characteristics like contradictions. He discusses four exceptional features of artistic judgments on the beautiful those he consequently deals with the inspiring. He calls them 'moments' and according to his major classifications these are prearranged in vague ways.

In Kant's first moment there are two types of interest. He defined interest as a connection to action and real desire. Moreover interest is a decisive link to the true existence of a particular thing. First interest is by way of sensations in the agreeable and next is by way of concepts in the good. Aesthetic judgment is free from these types of interests and the aesthetic judgment for itself, the real subsistence according to beautiful object is reasonably unrelated. Kant claims that the artistic judgments have to concern structure of an object like arrangement, shape, rhythm, etc. It does not consider sensible contents color, tone, etc. Rodolphe Gasché pointed out that, "natural beauty is superior to artificial beauty because of natural beauty pleases by itself" (Gasche, 2003, p. 177). The reason is that the second has a

---

[9] Mary A. McCloskey, *Kant's Aesthetic* (Albany: State University of New York Press, 1987).

profound link to the agreeable, and to interest. Through these arguments, Kant becomes the initiator of formalism in aesthetics related with modern philosophy. However his arguments regarding aesthetic judgments are probably the most criticized concepts by following philosophers. This conflict is resulted to take in fine art as significant aspect as well as the part of nature. Kant's argument is discarded by philosophers like Nietzsche and Freud and Hegel, according to them all art can be understood as associated to will because of all arts are the part of culture.

In his second moment of Critique of the Power of Judgment, Kant claims that aesthetic judgments perform universally; it engages anticipation on the agreement of others. This universality is separated first from the mere prejudice of judgments because that is not universal. Ted Honderich remarks that, "Kant's central notion is that judgments of particular objects beauty which is not merely agreeable" (Honderich, 2005, p. 10). By the third moment Kant introduces the problem of purpose and purposiveness behind the search for beauty. He considered that an object's purpose is according to its derivation or purposiveness. Kant argues that the beautiful is identified with an object's purposive, but it is not based any specific purpose. He clarifies that beauty of a thing should not measure with utility and perfection because it is always purposive. A purpose may be the set of exterior purposes or the internal one. In external case, utility of the object is the criterion of judgment, in the internal, condition judgment is based on object's perfection. Thus according to beauty in nature, Kant stands with purposive; it is completely related with individual's sense of judgment on a particular thing. Ruth Chadwick states that, "Beauty is not in the object but in the response of an individual to the object and the harmony between mans cognitive faculties and the world" (Honderich, 2005, p. 8). However there is no ascertainable purpose with respect of his determinate cognition behind the beauty. In fact, Kant describes as beauty is enjoyable it is defined as a sensitivity that takes place on the realization of a purpose, or no less than the identification of purposiveness.

Stecker points out:

> "On Kant's view, even after dependent beauty has been introduced, it is wrong to suppose that art is valuable for the knowledge it provides or even that it makes an important contribution to knowledge. Art is to be valued for the pleasure it affords us. This pleasure, however, is not sensuous faculties

that give us knowledge. Hence, aesthetic pleasure requires the exercise of the intellect." [10]

Kant seems to argue that works of art should be treated as dependent beauties. He states:

> "If, however, the object is presented as a product of art, and such is to be declared beautiful, then, seeing that art always presupposes an end [...] a concept of what the thing is intended to be must first of all be laid at its basis [...] in estimating a beauty of art the perfection of the thing must be also taken into account."[11]

Kant argues that the purposiveness of art is further complicated concept connected with the ascetics. It is true that art works may have particular purposes given by the artists while their production. Often an artist aims to express a certain feel to his creation, or certain idea. Here Kant says that these feel or idea cannot be enough to create beauty for the object of an artist. The aesthetic judgment is only possible by the separation of real purposes of an artist from his artificial figure. The intention for the beauty of the beautiful occurs by the positive judgment of a person without any assumption. Kant writes that a judgment does not pursue or make an influential concept behind the beauty. In short, he forms idea of 'common sense' by his four 'Moments of the Beautiful'. Rachel Zuckert pointed out that, "Kant's ascetic judgments are justified on the grounds that they employ an idea or feeling between the faculties" (Zuckert, 2007, p. 336). Kant also suggests that common sense, in order to possible, the identical with the same faculties as normal cognition. That explains those characteristics of human beings make possible natural and determinative experience. Kant declares that the faculties are simply in agreement rather than shaping determinate cognition.

---

[10] Robert Stecker. *Free Beauty, Dependent Beauty, and Art*. Journal of aesthetic Education, Vol. 21, No.1 (Spring, 1987), pp.89-99

[11] Immanuel Kant. *Critique of Judgment*. Trans. Werner S. Plubar. Indianopolis, Ind.: Heckett, 1987

Final Considerations

Beauty seems to me to have different views for Kant, Hegel and Adorno. I have tried to show the conflicting views of these authors towards the idea of the beautiful in what natural beauty and art beauty are concerned. Hegel absolutely finds out beauty in fine art and he keeps out the beauty of nature. He argues that beauty in nature is formless and there are no criteria to analyze it. He again affirms that a simple art work pass through individuals mind is superior to any creation of nature. His concept 'content' in art works is called by him as the 'Idea' and it is considered as truth. Adorno considers realistic beauty happens through the ability of a person to access the object in its distinctiveness. He was inspired by Kant so one can see this influence in his notion. Adorno acquired some support from Kant for his idea of beauty. Hegel considered spirit is the important feature of works of art. Against Hegelian concept, Adorno claim that spirit is too significant factor in the creation of natural beauty. Kant discusses four exceptional features of artistic judgments on the beautiful. He explains that the beautiful is recognized with purposive, but not any specific purpose. Art works are made with particular purposes given by the artists while their production.

I proposed to attempt at least to suggest the reasons for, if not to reconcile, opinions as widely different as the ones presented in the essay and, at the same time, to offer a less impetuous and more carefully substantiated analysis of these theorists. The art works attached represent to me the best representation of what beauty is therefore proposed or if not, stated.

Work Cited

Adorno, Theodor. *Aesthetic Theory*, trans. C. Lenhardt (New York: Routledge & Kegan Paul, 1984)

Adorno, T. W. *Aesthetic Theory*. Continuum International Publishing Group, 1997

Beardsley, M. C. *Aesthetics from Classical Greece to the Present: A Short History*. University of Alabama Press, 1975

Carritt, E. F. *The Theory of Beauty*. Taylor & Francis, 1962

Davies, S., Kathleen Marie Higgins & Robert Hopkins. *A Companion to Aesthetics*. 2nd Edition. John Wiley and Sons, 2009

Desmond, William. *Art and the Absolute: A Study of Hegel's Aesthetics.*(Albany: State University of New York Press, 1986)

Eysteinsson, A. & Vivian Liska. *Modernism*, Volume 1. John Benjamins Publishing Company, 2007

Gasche, R. *The Idea of Form: Rethinking Kant's Aesthetics*. Stanford University Press, 2003

Hegel, Georg Wilhelm Friedrich. *Aesthetics: Lectures on Fine Art*. Trans. T. M. Knox and W. Miller. Oxford: Oxford University Press, 1975

Hegel, Georg Wilhelm Friedrich. "*The Philosophy of Fine Arts*," in *Philosophies of Art and Beauty*, ed. Albert Hofstadter and Richard Kughns (New York: The Modern Library, 1964)

Honderich, T. *The Oxford Companion to Philosophy*. 2nd Edition. Oxford University Press, 2005

Kant, Immanuel. *Critique of Judgment*. Trans. Werner S. Plubar. Indianopolis, Ind.: Heckett, 1987

McCloskey, Mary A. *Kant's Aesthetic* (Albany: State University of New York Press, 1987)

Nicholls, A. & Martin Liebscher. *Thinking the Unconscious: Nineteenth-Century German Thought*. Cambridge University Press, 2010

Nicholsen, S. W. *Exact Imagination, Late Work: On Adorno's Aesthetics*. MIT Press, 1999

Schaper, Eva. "*Free and Dependent Beauty.*" Chapter 3 of *Studies in Kant's Aesthetics* (Edinburgh: Edinburgh University Press, 1979)

Stecker, Robert. *Free Beauty, Dependent Beauty, and Art*. Journal of aesthetic Education, Vol. 21, No.1 (Spring, 1987), pp.89-99

Sukla, A. C. *Art and Experience*. Greenwood Publishing Group, 2003

Zuckert, R. *Kant on Beauty and Biology: An Interpretation of the 'Critique of Judgment'*. Cambridge University Press, 2007

"Landscape with the Marriage of Isaac and Rebecca" (1648 by Claude Lorraine)

"The Descent from the Cross" (1611 by Rubens)

12